I0478577

Debited, Credited and Accounted

Debited, Credited and Accounted

Bridging Human Behavior
and Accounting

Maria Victoria Q. Caparas

ISBN-13: 978-1490599137
ISBN-10: 1490599134

To all the hardworking accountants,
especially to University of the East
BSBA Accounting '87.

CONTENTS

ACKNOWLEDGMENTS

This book has been largely inspired by my first blog entitled "Shifting Perspectives: Musings of an Accountant-turned-Human Behavior Enthusiast."

I would like to express my gratitude to my sister Dang Diaz who introduced me to blogging in 2005.

Special thanks to everyone who read my blog, especially those who followed it, commented on it, or sent me their feedback.

Last but not the least, I would like to express my sincere gratitude to my editor, Josephine Teves.

1 CAREER CHANGE

I hardly knew anyone who has not had some form of career shift in life. The change could be partial, total, or radical. There is that friend doctor who ventured into the food business. I am acquainted with a computer programmer who became a photographer and an engineer who turned to acting. I could also include the great number of career women who became homemakers.

I myself experienced a career change from accounting to education. With a college degree in accounting but with only a couple of years of professional practice as a CPA, I still do some bookkeeping for my own finances, and I advise my colleagues and friends regarding their personal and/or business accounts. I can teach basic accounting at a moment's notice and as for the more advanced accounting subjects, perhaps after a few days of teaching preparation.

Needless to say, accounting is deeply ingrained in me that I retain its many lessons – frameworks, principles, and concepts. I have found it handy to understand and explain many occurrences in daily living. I still work with an accountant's mind and eyes. As examples, I calculate the unproductive man-hours in many office meetings. I notice lacks of internal control in a grocery store transaction. I even foresee advanced asset impairment in a young person's stress-laden work style.

Thus, accounting is a very useful tool that a career shift does not oblige me to abandon. Unconsciously or by force of habit, I always take it out of the toolbox to employ when needed. It could happen likewise with the aforementioned doctor who has started a restaurant. Her choice of menu and frequency of offering could be influenced by her knowledge of food effects on the body's immune system. Further, she can also easily bring with her to the household her office skills in planning and organizing.

Obviously when one is in the thick of work, a tool is no more than a tool, like a carpenter who sees his hammer as a hammer and only a hammer. Likewise, the daily bookkeeping and reporting, the tedious sameness of information analysis, the invariable defense of generally-accepted accounting principles to non-accountants who question them—these could generate in the accountant a very restricted perspective of business such that he/she does not see far beyond the books of accounts, balance sheet, or income statement. Neither does the available training help to enlarge his/her vision of business if the options are limited to accounting skills and professional updates.

In this regard, I was reminded of a middle-aged woman who participated in a human resource management course that I facilitated. Working as a chief accountant in a medium-sized business, she stood up and asked me the typical question about how to manage a boss. She enumerated all the tasks and projects she had at hand in contrast to those of her boss, who had less workload and usually out of the office, playing golf or travelling. I advised her to recall how many deals were closed by her boss, or in general, how many business contracts came through in the past three months. She was reflective after that, and I simply hoped that she got a broader view of the organization and the diversity of roles and functions.

Undeniably, there is no business that can survive without an accountant to provide the necessary information for management decisions. But as a useful tool, accounting has its obvious limitations that are keenly perceived more by the non-accountants. To wit, the business cannot thrive with it only as a trade tool. It cannot measure and record everything that sustains a business. And although the debits might equal the credits, the employees may be highly dissatisfied.

I am not in any way endorsing "human resource accounting" which gained popularity in the '70s along with the upsurge of interest for the competitive value of effective people management. (Now a revival is seen in the form of "human capital accounting."). First, I think it will be a nightmare to produce and implement another set of generally accepted accounting principles regarding valuation of human resources. Second, any valuation can easily backfire on the people themselves in poor economic times, or downsizing strategies. I sense that there will still be a lot of number-crunching in these revived or new paradigms although not within the accountants' comfort zone of accuracy.

What I am proposing is a bridge between the hard and soft sides of business, such that accountants can increase their territorial span without abandoning their own terrain completely. I am not comfortable with the idea that accountants need to trash their technical know-how, and learn the art of managing human capital to move higher within the corporate ladder. If that is the case, the heads of the HR or personnel departments would be the best candidates for the CEO post, wouldn't they?

I prefer synergisms than radical shifts. The synergistic approach respects the past and makes the future less intimidating. It seeks to enrich rather than impoverish because what is still useful is not discarded but developed further and made relevant beyond its boundaries. Synergisms can also reaffirm the original chosen path after it has been examined from a broader perspective.

In aiming to make linkages, *Debited, Credited and Accounted* may not only point out accounting's weaknesses but it will also exalt its strengths. For as you will read in these lines and in between, I am still enthused by accounting. I wish especially the new entrants to the profession a comprehensive vision of business management that will enable them to effectively manage an entire business (or at least, a profit center) and also lead a balanced life...as balanced as the books of accounts that they keep.

2 THE ORDER OF ACCOUNTANTS

My brother is the first CPA in the family. I was actually inspired to take up accounting in the University of the East because of him. He came home one day giving us the good news that he would only pay half of the tuition for the following semester because of his final grades. I terribly liked the idea— getting free tuition by merit— that I never applied for admissions to any other university.

Anyway, back to my brother. He assigned me some bookkeeping for the family finances at a certain period. Much to my consternation after the time and effort I had spent, he commented upon seeing my worksheet that he was very confused with it. I looked at my worksheet again and compared it with a previous one he did. To my shame, his was far neater than mine. He had all the accurate titles, bold and italic fonts for emphasis, as well as single and double underlines.

If you choose to be in accounting, see if you really have the personality for it. It is most suited for the ones who can live with many rules and regulations, less ambiguity and more conformity. (Even the so-called "creative accounting" has its limits and risks in the context of accounting and reporting standards.)

Does it mean that someone who is imaginative or creative should be discouraged from aspiring to be an accountant? Definitely not. I do not know yet of any accounting school that includes personality tests in its selection process. But acquiring the habit of order in and out of the classroom or workplace will really come in handy if you wish to thrive in the profession.

Order includes not just knowing how to arrange things but actually arranging them in their proper place or category. The order of liquidity is one classic example. The balance sheet is organized according to the order of decreasing liquidity. The most liquid asset which is cash is on top of the list of accounts. You may see down in the list the fixed assets or long-term assets that will take time to convert to cash. Needless to say, if the balance sheet is for your personal use only, you may list the accounts in any arrangement you prefer and no one will stop you.

Knowing yourself and your habits will help you see if you are inclined to the order of the accountants. Your inclination towards the practice of order will make it easy for you to remember and follow some accounting formats and standards without much emphasis for memorization and constant referencing or searching into your lecture notes and books. For example, do you organize your clothes in your closet by order of type or by color? Do you arrange the money notes in your wallet by color or value? Is your handwriting legible? Are the contents of your school bag arranged in a sort of system? Do you always plan what you will study after school or over the weekend?

Nevertheless, discounting the level of knowledge, it may be worthy to dismiss the idea that those who are typically disorganized and unsystematic cannot be accountants. All things being equal, they may encounter greater challenges than the orderly ones in applying some accounting practices that demand a lot of systematic calculations and order. However, it can be perceived that this challenge is not a permanent impediment. A student can always strive to put order in his/her daily life inasmuch as he/she is obliged to practice it in the technical world of accountancy work.

3 DOUBLE ENTRY AND ROLE MODELS

Accounting keeps your feet on the ground. When you receive something, it makes you reflect and ask yourself: "Is this mine or do I owe anyone for this?" Imagine finding 1,000 pesos in a clean envelope among your personal belongings. Unless you are really wont to scatter money everywhere in your home, you would stop, search your memory and ask: "Owed or owned?"

Accounting for a business takes on a two-sided nature which is reflected in the double-entry accounting system. Learn the following equation, by heart:

Assets = Liabilities + Owner's Equity

Thus, the double entry of the 1000 pesos would look like these in three different scenarios:

a. $1000 = 1000 + 0$ (*if the money was lent to me*)

b. 1000 = 0 + 1000 (*if the money was paid to me in exchange for what I sold*).

Note that this is a shortcut because I could have recognized a sales income first before closing my profit to owner's equity. At year-end, I will close all income accounts to retained earnings which are a source of owner's equity.

c. 1000-1000=0 + 0 (*if I honestly searched for the owner who lost it and surrendered the money to him/her*).

Piece of cake? I could imagine some students shouting "Nosebleed!" Okay, so here is another way to understand the double entry system.

Think of a role model, someone you want to imitate because his/her behavior is particularly appealing to you. And imagine that someone lives in the house beside yours with a wall separating your two houses.

Think of the wall as the "=" in the accounting equation, and you live at the left side of the wall. If your role model tries to acquire a certain hobby like gardening, you would do as well, right? So an addition to the right side of the equation must also need an addition to the left side of it.

If your role model decides to quit a vice, like smoking 16 cigarettes a day, you would also follow suit. This means that a deduction from the right side of the equation must also require a deduction from the left side of the "=" sign.

Then suppose that you are trying to impress your role model by showing off a lawn mower. However, he does not notice you, and he keeps on manually cutting the grass. So you decide to sell off the lawn mower. This means that an addition to the left side of the equation that has no counterpart addition to the right side will have to be cancelled out by a subtraction from the left side.

Now, imagine this: You were surprised one day that your role model came home driving a sleek, expensive car. You were greatly tempted to buy a new car likewise but your finances were tight. Fortunately, he realized that the car was a little over the top. He rectified, sold the car, and started to look for a cheap sober type.

Applying this to the double entry system, the addition to the right side of the equation is neutralized by a deduction, if there is no complementary addition to the left side of the "=" sign.

Do you understand double entry a little bit more? Don't give up easily if you still don't. Try mastering the double entry concept using the given examples or any other ones you can find. Or better yet, I recommend that you find a role model for persistence as this is such a fundamental lesson in accounting that if you do not grasp it, you will advance to the higher accounting subjects with much greater difficulty, or might not even be able to advance at all.

4 DEBITS, CREDITS AND REALISM

I heard a friend praising another mutual friend for her effective multitasking skills. I was able to conclude that "something's gotta give." And when I did get the chance to examine one task output, I was correct. The distinguished accomplishments were not as perfect in all areas as they seemed. "Am I being cynical?" I think I am just being a real, and I must say, I owe it in the basic Accounting rule that says "debits must equal credits".

Think of credits as your sources of funds like owner's capital and loans from creditors. Then think of debits as uses of funds like assets, costs and expenses.

Let's say, one gets a loan of 24 hours. (We can even say it is an equity of 24 hours but once you are in the streets, you can never be 100% sure that you will have the next 24 hours to enjoy. I am not 100% sure so I will settle for the "loan".) If you tell me that you have high grades, you also keep your boarding house clean and tidy, maintain your wonderful relationships with others and you are an active student leader, then it may be worthy to assume that you are performing those duties 24/7.

Applying accounting terms on your ordinary life, it may be safe to assume that for debits to equal credits, something's "gotta give". For example, look into how many hours you are sleeping or taking meals. Have you missed out on important family occasions in the past months? Are you up-to-date with national events?

Debits equal credits. Apply it every day. Think of your physical body as equity. As infants, we were given a small capital and as the years go by, with the individual decisions we make as regards basic necessities, we have increased or decreased our net worth. Such "net worth" naturally helps us to expand and explore on things that we formerly think we cannot do.

But since we are free rational beings, we can go for greater achievements ("purchase assets") more than we can with our present net worth. It's as if we make salary advances, as we are always confident that we can pay them back in the next pay day. Hopefully, the next pay day comes for us.

My blockmate in Accounting, Arlyn hit the nail in the head when she wrote me "I go for the basic idea in Accounting: *debit always equals credit*. There should always be a balance between work life and family or personal life. Most of us are working so hard to earn a living forgetting what we are really working for, often neglecting ourselves and our families."

5 BANK RECONCILIATION

I will share with you why the monthly reconciliation of book and bank accounts is one of the easiest exercises I learned in college. But first of all, let me describe a little of what reconciliation in accounting means, which is not very far from how the dictionary defines it: "the act of restoring to harmony."

If a company has money in the bank, it should regularly reconcile its cash in bank balance with the amount that the bank says it has, according to the monthly bank statements that they mail to the company (now you can get the bank statements online). The reason is that sometimes the book balance will differ from the bank balance. Hence there is a need to reconcile the two amounts, and find out the reason for the difference to be able to act upon it promptly (for example, adjust the book balance or inform the bank if it has to be the one to make adjustments).

I remember three methods of doing reconciliation. The first is book-to-bank balance, which means that you start with the book balance to arrive at the unadjusted bank balance. The second is bank-to-book balance, which means that you start with the bank balance to arrive at the unadjusted book balance. The third is the adjusted balances method, which means that you start with both balances to arrive at the correct balance for both book and bank.

The usual reconciling items which will not require any book entry are the deposits in transits and outstanding checks. It can happen that at month-end the company already records some receipts that will still be deposited the following banking day. Hence these are deposits in transit to the bank. The company will expect that the bank will credit this upon receipt of the deposit the next banking day which is already the following month. Outstanding checks are those released by the company but have not yet been presented to the bank or have not yet cleared the bank.

You don't get it? Okay, let's go to the working assumptions and hope you can find your way from there.

The first must-have assumption is that the bank can make mistakes. Even nowadays when many bank transactions are automated, there can still be errors like a single deposit recorded twice.

The second must-have assumption is that the company can also make mistakes for a variety of reasons. The person handling the cash-in-bank ledger can erroneously record a check of 980 to 890 (due to inattention, poor eyesight, waking up at the wrong side of bed, etc.)

The third must-have assumption is that the bank and book may not always be perfectly synchronized unless the transactions are online and in real time. They are not obliged to synchronize with each other every minute, as they are two independent entities. For example, the bank will deduct regular charges before the company gets to know it, and the company will pay out a check which will be presented to the bank two months after.

The fourth and last must-have assumption is that reconciliation saves time and effort if you do it monthly. Especially if you have many daily bank transactions, it will already be tedious, if not more difficult, to do the reconciliation after more than one month.

Take these lessons to your personal life and relationships and see how they could be equally relevant.

6 TRIAL BALANCE

Preparing a trial balance at any time during the year is a particular precaution for bookkeepers. It reveals any disparity between total debits and total credits which could be due to errors in journalizing or posting in the general ledger. And at year-end, a trial balance precedes the preparation of adjusting entries. As a student, I simply think of the trial balance as an essential compulsory step before making the balance sheet: "try it first if it will balance."

There's no harm in trying...now. I keep telling that to friends who tell me their dreams of doing something different once they finish their deadlines. One said that in her vacation (for which she has not put a definite date yet) she would love to learn how to cook all her favorite dishes. Another would love to attend painting classes. A third would explore all the Apple apps. Invariably, I advised each one: try it now, do it now. Be an expert in one dish this month. Get the painting course schedule this weekend. Go to a Wi-Fi hotspot and tap App Store.

For someone in a workaholic lifestyle to get an actual experience of change is critical. First of all, it is not easy to get out of the vicious cycle where a deadline gives rise to one or several others. Second, doing something different from the usual work is treading on unchartered waters. The risk-averse would not want to feel they are not doing anything at all. It would be disloyalty to their calling as workaholics if they don't do any work at all. Third, what would the others say? They might get the impression that the work commitment is waning.

There are ways to help them ease up and strike the trial balance. One would be through vicarious experience. I talk constantly, albeit briefly, about non-work adventures of mutual friends. I would categorize these as stories. Another would be information, like facilitating that someone never forgets about the painting class. I would email info on traditional and virtual classes that I "chanced upon" the internet one day. Also a way is actual experience. I would help my friend jumpstart her rest right there and then if possible. If she only mentions a crash course in something I know, I will give her my five minutes, not more because a workaholic tends to think that she is impertinently taking the time of another workaholic.

I know if I am successful in my attempts for the workaholics' trial balance by their facial expression (at the very least, they are listening and not thinking of work), email response (they took the time to reply on a non-work issue), or an update even from a third party how they are making a headway in their dreams (now, that is a non-subjective judgment).

I am convinced that trial balance will result to adjustments, sooner or later.

7 YEAR-END ADJUSTMENTS

At year-end, companies close the general ledger after making the necessary adjustments. Balance sheet accounts are not closed, unlike profit and loss accounts which begin with zero at the beginning of the year.

There may be adjustments that can be tough for many accounting students. (I recall our accounting professor always used a timeline to establish the necessary adjusting entries.) Perhaps relating the adjusting entries to real life situations may help ease any perplexity about those difficulties.

To start with, during the year, the human body may suffer deterioration, sometimes unnoticed. Perhaps you don't realize how much and how many tissues and cells have been damaged (not to exclude the brain neurons that became less efficient, muscle tones that declined, bones that lost density, etc.). Even then, it is unrealistic to assume that you will start the New Year with the same quality of body systems as you started this year, unless your body is healthy enough, and repairs and damages have been considered enough.

Realizing the possibility of asset deterioration over time is also called for in business. Thus, company accountants make adjusting entries in order to recognize the depreciation of fixed assets. They know that depreciation is a cost to the business, hence it should be debited. On the other side of the equation, there is no outright credit or deduction to Fixed Assets. Following the historical cost principle, we need to report and present fixed assets in the balance sheet at their original costs. Instead, the credit should be in Accumulated Depreciation account, which is a contra asset account—it is shown in the balance sheet as a deduction to Fixed Assets.

Adjusting entries involving revenues will depend on what entries were originally made upon receipt of the payment from the clients. If revenue was credited on June 1 for a service that will be rendered to the client for 12 months, then an adjusting entry is necessary on December 31 to decrease (debit) the revenue and to recognize (credit) the liability to continue to render the service from January to May next year. It's like someone has a predisposition to be presumptuous and he/she makes a New Year's resolution to be more humble and to keep one's commitments.

If a liability was recognized on June 1 upon receipt of the client's fees by crediting unearned revenue, then an adjusting entry is necessary on December 31 to decrease (debit) the liability and increase (credit) the revenue for the service already rendered from

June 1 to December 31 this year. This time, we can imagine that someone has a predisposition towards being too timid and cautious. He/she then makes a New Year's resolution be more confident that the service will be rendered well and the client will be very satisfied.

Adjusting entries involving expenses will also depend on what entries were originally made upon payment to suppliers. If expense was debited on July 1 for an office rent of 12 months, then an adjusting entry is necessary on December 31 to recognize that there is a prepayment and decrease (credit) the expense. The prepayment is an asset because the company keeps the benefit of the rented space until June 30 of the following year. That's a great way to end the year in a spirit of thanksgiving.

If a prepaid asset was recognized on July 1 upon an advance payment of rent for 12 months, then an adjusting entry is necessary on December 31 to decrease the asset (credit) and recognize a rental expense (debit) for the actual use of the rented space for the past six months. So we end the year by being honest with what we really possess.

8 ASSETS AND LIABILITIES

An asset is defined as "an item of value owned". In accounting, this definition already includes two tests for an asset to be considered an accounting asset. The first is if it has value such that an income can generate from its use. An example would be a truck that delivers vegetables for sale from Baguio to Manila, or the cash that will pay for the next delivery of items for resale. The second test is ownership. Although the North Luzon Expressway has value to me if I am in a trucking business, I cannot consider it my asset because I do not own it.

On the other hand, a liability is defined as "something for which one is liable", a debt, a drawback or a disadvantage. In accounting, a liability is a debt, something that puts a claim to your assets. Thus, we do not confuse the books by categorizing an asset as a liability or vice versa. You can't say that your factory is a debt if you really own it. A loan is not owned, but is owed to the lender.

However in a non-accounting sense, my delivery truck can already be a liability, i.e. a drawback, if it is always in the repair shop. Because of the downtime, I can incur more costs (e.g. delayed goods, angry customers) rather than earn income. My credit card (or bank payable), even if it is a liability by itself, can actually have tremendous value for me such that I can purchase anything anytime even with zero cash on hand.

Does it mean that accounting categories do not make sense? Not the least. They actually put order and neatness in an otherwise topsy-turvy world of business. Just enter a textile store in Divisoria to get a glimpse of the accounting challenge. Imagine how entrepreneurs will survive if accountants do not give them orderly reports and financial statements regularly. That explains why categories are an important beginning. The next key step is to maximize the assets and/or minimize the negative consequences of liabilities. Perhaps the experience of a student can illustrate this point:

One of the pleasures of a teacher is to meet former students and hear how they have fared in the world of work. I had that satisfaction some time ago. An alumna invited me for a chat over coffee. Immediately after college graduation, she was hired by a multinational as a management trainee for three years. But just a year after she began her contract, she was already being groomed for greater responsibilities. Then, officially her contract was shortened obviously for passing with flying colors.

I was not totally surprised with the good news. This alumna whom I was lucky to mentor for a mini-thesis was the type who always walked the extra mile. Given one instruction, she would spend those periods in between consultations with me having all the initiative and diligence to move ahead. She knew how to obey intelligently. With her, I felt my advices were not really needed but she would come for mentoring sessions with eager face and hands. She listened very attentively, took notes actively, clarified doubts with the simplicity of a learner, asked questions with the sincerity of one who is zealous to be helped.

Back in school, I shared the news of her success and a colleague commented: "With beauty and brains like hers, she can go places with little effort." Perhaps yes, but not always. I have also met equally charming and smart students but in interactions in school, I can see that they themselves are putting a limit to their own progress. It is evident in their outputs, in their presence in the classroom, in their answers, etc. They can do more, but they just don't. Success is within reach but at the same time unreachable.

Going back to my former mentee, I find her breaking a certain mold of a product of a broken family. She is a survivor. She has a vision of what she wants to be, within the constraints of the family, school, and the relationship she got into. Given her academic track record and incipient outstanding career performance, I am pretty sure she will get there, unless she suffers a radical change of perspective in work and life.

It is obvious that my mentee started college with an initial asset of intelligence and she maximized it by diligence in all school work requirements and even going the extra mile, in exceeding my expectations as both teacher and mentor. She also had an initial liability of family disunity. But if it did affect her, it did not show in her high academic performance. Hence I can say that she minimized the effect of that liability which, for other students in similar circumstances, can impair their ability to focus and deliver work expectations.

9 PAST DUE MOVIES

I am not really a movie enthusiast. In fact, a friend who is an expert in films could have literally strangled me one day when I said I watched "Schindler's List" in one hour since I simply browsed it (that is, using fast forward button) from beginning to end.

Vacation time usually gives me the advantage to watch past due movies. I use the term "past due" like in accounting – something that is owed and the deadline to claim it has fallen due some time ago. So it is payback time—time to watch Peter Jackson's Lord of the Rings: the Fellowship of the Ring. Not that I have not seen it at all. But I freely contracted the obligation to watch it again leisurely, in a number of viewing times to really capture all the symbolisms spread out in that Tolkien masterpiece.

The "Fellowship of the Ring" begins with a narration of the origin of the One Ring, from the forging of the great rings, to the surreptitious forging of a master ring and its loss in the cut hand of Sauron in the battlefield of Middle-earth, and to its discovery by Gollum and Bilbo Baggins. The movie centers on the formation of the fellowship with a mission to accompany Frodo Baggins to drop the Ring of Power to the flames of Mount Doom where it was forged. It ends precisely when Frodo and Sam could view their final destination, expressing the hope that they would reunite with their former companions again.

Blame my reflective mood on the quiet atmosphere I choose during vacation, which led to my seeing the symbolism of death throughout the film. Where does death come out?

It's quite easy to point out from the opening scenes - the disappearance of Sauron as soon as his finger with the ring was cut, or the death of Isildor after coveting the Ring, or the many casualties in the featured wars.

But was death their end? Sauron appeared again as his Ring was reawakened with its powers after 3000 years. The day of Isildur's death is alive in the memories of elves and men as the day the reign of noble Kings ended with the failure of the strength of Men. The orcs were dug from their graves and were commissioned by Saruman to bring him the one Halfling that carries a thing of great value.

However, even if death is the end, it is also the beginning of another life that seems to be much more potent than the first. For Sauron, it is now a more tremendously fearful crusade to get back the Ring. For Isildur, it was a legacy that brought shame, but it restored a new life of courage for his descendant Aragorn, even if his cousin Boromir has lost hope.

The particular scene of the remains of Boromir in regalia in a boat that leads towards the East portrays death as a step to one's definitive destiny. At his dying moment, he reconciled with Aragorn and gave him his esteem as "my brother, my captain, my King". Aragorn promised him that with all his strength, the White City will not fall into ruin, and Boromir seemed to have died hopeful.

I find fiction as having a peculiar way of never intending to proclaim the truth as other sciences do, but somehow it gets to do it. If this Tolkien classic does not really declare to anyone that death is the end, at least it could raise the doubt if death really is. It's like asking at the end of a very captivating movie: "That's it?" expecting that there's going to be a sequel.

I think of past due movies to understand past due receivables which are sometimes considered already as bad debts. There are many lessons on credit control, risk management, accounting system glitches, and customer relations that the company can learn from the analysis of past due accounts.

From my experience as a finance manager, I realized that there might still be gold in past due accounts. So I must be careful in writing them off as bad debts. For example, a few days after assuming the post, I saw a huge list of tuition fees receivable that were past due in a postgraduate program. I called some of the students' companies myself and was pleased to get a number of positive responses. One said a check for us was already stale, a miscommunication perhaps. Hence, the collection of a new check was scheduled for the collector. Another company regretted the omission on their part and promised to process the check payment soon. Of course, there were a few angry debtors who said they did not get the value promised to them.

Past due movies or past due collectibles: I keep the hope to claim benefits from them someday, somehow.

10 DEPRECIATION AND REST

Someone asked me: from what disease do accountants suffer that others don't? I blurted out in succession: stress, insomnia, a disease of the heart or liver... And Joker's answer was depreciation. Amusing.

But in defense of all accountants who are still my colleagues as I have not totally abandoned the profession, I believe that everyone depreciates regardless of profession. In accounting, depreciation means the physical wear and tear and obsolescence of fixed assets. In real life, I relate it to greater susceptibility to stress and tension, deceleration of mental faculties, weakening of physical strength, muscular atrophy, or aching of joints.

In this regard, depreciation of a human being can be a humbling experience. It makes you realize that you are not an almighty being who can live long years in an eternal springtime. At the same time, it makes you wonder at the genius of that great Technician who determined the expiry dates as well as the proper care and maintenance of your every cell, tissue and organ.

Take precaution. Have regular rest not only every weekend but also for longer days every year to regain strength of body as well as of spirit, to remove oneself away from the maddening crowd and the feverish rhythm of city life, to rediscover one's uniqueness as it might have gotten lost and became anonymous somewhere along the way as a consumer, a statistic in population surveys, a user of quickly changing technologies or a follower of fashion.

Go out and meet Mother Nature. She is a great host for periodic maintenance.

11 DEBT AND FILIAL PIETY

Asian societies traditionally have a strong culture of intergenerational support. Filial piety presupposes that children are indebted to their parents and are obliged to reciprocate them. Children, especially the eldest son (and his wife), are expected to have a sense of gratitude towards their parents and the obligation to provide care for them in their old age. This filial piety is much less pronounced in Western societies.

A Spanish professor in one of his books likened piety to being in a situation of debt that one will not be able to pay off fully, no matter how much has been paid. It's like having a perpetual bank overdraft. I did not take this negatively, being an Asian. But what called my attention is the effective application of finance concepts to a cultural trait. It stuck to me.

I would simply qualify that the debt is contracted freely, no matter how strong the influence (or indoctrination) of society and family may be. Children will find ways to get out of it when they don't want it.

And they can pay back, but the quantity and the quality (i.e. attitude, disposition, behavior) of discharging the obligation depend much on personal freedom. Thus, some Asian governments with problematic elderly care situations find the need to reinforce filial piety through values formation.

When humans can impose a debt obligation, God is a lender who does not demand payback. He is not the man in motorcycle making his rounds daily collecting debts. He is the most powerful yet hardly remembered creditor.

12 GROSS WAGES

There is a certain expression, especially from the young ones, that calls my attention. They can say "that's gross!" to anything that they find more or less disgusting—whether it's a plate of food, a photo, a story narration, or a gesture. I wonder how they will comprehend "gross wages or salaries" when they encounter it in accounting books or in their pay stubs. Shall I tell you when gross can really be gross?

When an employer berates a worker in front of co-workers and customers, I think it's gross. Does the employer assume that the gross wages he pays entitle him to demand total submission of hands and reputation? I recall seeing a supervisor scold a staff behind a stall in a food court. Besides the fact that talking before food is not hygienic, scolding someone before a wide-eyed public lacks refinement. I lost appetite and left the table.

When an employer pays a worker the minimum wage and expects not only the task accomplishment but also putting all of the worker's intellectual capacity, love for work, and loyalty to the company, I think it's gross. Is there equity in giving little in exchange for the entire universe?

When an employee holds back his intellectual capacity or refuses to develop when the company provides him with the necessary training and formation, I think it's gross. He could look for an employer who pays for career plateaus.

When an employee renders strictly his written duties in a heartless or soulless manner, I think it's gross. What amount of salary does he believe can rightfully lay claim to his dedication? Perhaps the company should rather pay mercenaries who are straightforward with who they are and what they can do.

13 COSTING A LIFE

Cost accounting was one of my favorite subjects in college. I would acquire a certain sense of fulfillment just by arriving at a product's unit cost or total cost of sales. I felt it empowering to be able to make critical decision-making aided by the knowledge of the relevant costs and trade-offs. For example, cost accounting assists a manager to determine what production area he/she can control on cost or decide which product line is worth continuing or giving up.

Solving a textbook's illustrative exercises to master cost accounting can be tedious, but it was not difficult because it all seemed logical to me. It's like you cannot arrive at any other unit cost if you only follow the procedures and consider all relevant expenses. Put in all the materials, labor, and overhead that go into a job order or a distinct cost, then divide the total by the number of units produced and you get the unit cost. You can't go wrong. (I am over-simplifying perhaps, but this is not an accounting textbook, so bear with me.)

Decades after laboring on countless hypothetical costing exercises, I came across a problem that crossed the boundaries of costing logic and altered the predictability of decisions based on available cost information.

I have a friend, an expert in a specialized organ transplant. She began to build her practice in the country after spending years of specialization in several countries. In the process, she was presented a serious case of a two-year-old patient whom local facilities were not prepared to handle. My friend turned to her colleagues abroad. Unfortunately, her first foreign contacts did not accept the case. Henceforth, my friend contacted an equally competent hospital in another country. That hospital had many requirements before they could accept the young patient but their consultants were willing to come over to save her.

In the two weeks that my friend was negotiating everything—from the travel to the post-op care, I could sense that she was losing a lot of weight. Fortunately, she was able to make two local hospitals enter into a joint venture on the needed transplant, each one having distinct assets to contribute to this type of delicate surgery. To make the long story short, when the foreign consultants agreed to come over to help my friend perform the task, the patient had a seizure and the operation was postponed until further notice.

All's well that ends well. But I can't help being amused with all the calculations we did to help our friend. The cost of transferring the transplant operation from one country to another with all the paper works involved, the stress, the anguish and all, was admittedly too much for one professional to handle, even with all her technical skills and expertise. Are these entirely the doctor's concern or the family's? Some of us in the circle of friends actually discouraged her to carry further on, after the first hospital opted out. "It is not your responsibility anymore", we advised her. And when she decided to persist with the case, we helped her calculate the greater costs involved *vis-à-vis* the donations received so far by the patient's family.

In the end, the accountant in me has to admit that monetary cost is a useful tool to make decisions, but it is neither the only one nor the most relevant criterion. When saving a life, a whole gamut of unquantifiable factors like sentiments, duty and relationships could replace a perfectly logical decision with an "illogical" choice.

Perhaps, if I had seen the suffering patient and her desperate parents as my friend doctor would see them every day, my logic of calculations would have taken a different turn.

14 IN PRAISE OF VOLUME

Although accountants may also understand volume as the amount of space occupied by a three-dimensional object, they most often use volume in terms of quantity. For example, volume of output refers to quantity of production, and sales volume is the number of units sold. Needless to say, high volume is desirable if the price is low. When all other costs are stable, the more you sell the greater the profit. Praise be volume.

I will go back to the city by Sunday. There are still more book pages to leaf through, documentary films to watch, sites to see, and people to visit.

A relative sent a video of cable TV coverage of World Youth Day. (As this little vacation town is not reached by cable, she must have thought I was missing the event tremendously, and indeed I am). I am not new to it, as Manila was the site of the biggest gathering of the youth with Pope John Paul in 1995. I was there in Luneta Park with approximately 3-5 million people of all ages. (The figure could be higher or lower depending on the news agency covering the event).

Anyway, I particularly noted the comment from one of the anchorpersons covering the event. He said that WYD is "a renewal of faith." For once he felt that with a crowd of young people praying, singing, walking, etc. he is affirmed in his faith—that he is not alone.

Who would not want high volume or quantity? It already feels good to believe in something or to believe in nothing (which does not disqualify one from being a believer). It must certainly feel much better when millions more share your convictions, unless you are an avowed individualist.

15 WORK-IN-PROGRESS

In costing a manufacturing concern, work-in-progress is determined. It refers to the costs of materials, direct labor, and overhead that is in process of production at the end of an accounting period. It's like taking a photo of an assembly line and capturing the reality that some goods have not reached the end of the line.

I love taking this expression into ordinary conversations. One time, a good friend revealed at dinner table, "Avic said I am a work-in-progress." I would never know if she found that expression novel or hurting. But I think we all are, except that for a few, they might find it useful to make it explicit in their curriculum vitae.

She was applying for certification and also for a teaching work. The application process has many variables at play, including the bureaucracy and lack of professionalism in a certain government agency. Keen to get the certificate as an additional proof of competencies, she was also worried about delaying her job search. I recommended that she had to finalize her curriculum vitae for the job application, provided that she qualifies the relevant certification as "in process". I have read a number of resumes wherein educational achievements include postgraduate degrees described further as "pending thesis" or "year started to present".

Will the person who is fully convinced that he/she is a "finished product" please come forward to be recognized?

16 WORK AS A PERCENTAGE OF LIFE

Two college students came one day to interview me as part of their two-unit course called Work and Society. One question which got me thinking for minutes was this: how much percentage of your day does work occupy?

The answer really depends on what is meant by "work". If it is paid work and means of livelihood, then I spend on the average a third of my day (8 out of 24 hours). I say "on the average" because my productivity varies daily. One day I work more, another day I work less. But on the average, I believe I render to the company what is due to it.

If work means any activity of body and/or mind, add a couple of hours for cleaning the house and dishwashing after dinner.

If by work, I mean my profession, career, calling or pursuit, and then add a couple more for unpaid hours of personal study, exchanging views with people from whom I intend to learn, expanding my professional network through the internet, etc.

Work comprises really a big bulk of the day when it goes beyond the sense of employment.

The rest of the day transpires in the personal milieu. That includes sleep, meals, exercise, hygiene, reflection, prayer, and forging ties with people that matter.

The division of the day into work and life is actually fuzzy to me, outside any survey or research question. Just think, if I do not infuse enthusiasm into my work, it would be a drag. And if I don't exert effort to make relationships work, I would be miserable.

17 A TV PER ROOM

"Per" is a curious English word that occurs most frequently in accounting. It means "with respect to every member of a specified group" and can be replaced with "for each". In analysis of financial reports, "per" signals to you that you are working with a ratio, and the word can also be replaced with "divided by".

For example, earnings per share is equal to net income divided by total number of stock shares. If EPS is Php2, then it means that you have Php2 income for each stock. Other uses include market price per share, cost per square meter, sales margin per unit, etc. But the ratio or its computation is only worth something if it helps to reflect upon and analyze the realities that the numbers represent.

I have always wondered what motivates the practice of installing a TV per room in a house. Is it materialism (the more the richer)? Interior design (it's got to be part of the room, even a bathroom)? Fear of being alone (no one's home. I need company)? Boredom (anything on TV is more exciting than schoolwork)? Fear of silence (my conscience keeps nagging me)? Bad mood (I can't stand my siblings; I will keep to my room)?

In the United States, Vandewater and colleagues estimated an average of 2.5 televisions per household. In addition, 43% of children aged three to four years old have a television in their bedrooms. Rideout and colleagues found that over two-thirds of 8- to 18-year-olds have a TV in their bedroom. Vandewater described the common reasons of parents for this family policy: to allow the other family members to watch the shows they like and to keep the kids occupied.

It would be interesting to get hold of research studying the relationship between TV density (or the total number of TVs in a house) and the number of times in a week that a family goes out together or takes meals all at the same time, the academic standing of a TV freak, the eloquence of the TV viewer to speak in his/her mother tongue or a second language, the depth of conviction in social and political issues, the breadth of knowledge in national and international affairs.

Don't get me wrong. The television has also been useful for me - to get news around the world, to entertain oneself with a show that is worth the time, to practice a foreign language, to preview a video I'll show in class. But that's just about it. Perhaps I only need 20 minutes a day for the news. Hence, I do not need one in my bedroom. I can share it with my family, or it will become an intruder in my intimacy.

The times have indeed changed. When I visit my relatives in the province, I see each room including the dining room with a TV. It drains my persuasive power to request them to turn off the TV during lunch. I miss my childhood days when we only have a small TV (just one that can fit a car), and we would watch basketball matches together. I was already in college when we got a bigger, colored TV.

When I was younger, my siblings and I were repeatedly summoned to get inside the house by sunset. A friend told me that the new "millenians" need to be repeatedly summoned to get out of the house and play at least an hour daily, or they would be watching TV all day.

The more the merrier? It ultimately depends on what you mean by merriment.

18 IDEAL SIZE OF TWO

As of today, the Reproductive Health Law (Republic Act 10354) signed by the President in December 2012 is under a *status quo ante* order by the Supreme Court. It is as if the law is non-existent until the high court lifts the order or extends it after its expiry on July 17, 2013.

I wrote a blog on one of the provisions of the bill when it was still being debated in Congress. The ideal size of two children per family has been modified into "the number of children desired [by individuals and couples]." But the law still lacks an explicit commitment to assist couples in raising a small or big family through social and economic opportunities and resources.

I have just read the proposed Responsible Parenthood and Population Management Act of 2005 by the Congress. It puts two children as the ideal family size. It says that this number will not be imposed. However, the enviable privileges like scholarships attached to this ideal size would already be too good to be ignored by families.

Why two and not one? What about three? I would be interested to know the quality of brain power that produced the number.

Personally, I feel grateful that I, the third child, am alive. It's good that my parents did not make me feel an unwanted child and a burden. However, I did observe that having a third child to send to school was a tough call for my parents who were then government employees. So I worked hard to have high grades to get scholarships in college and postgraduate schools. I also helped out in my family finances by doing part-time work as clerk or assistant vendor in a grocery store, and selling quails or quail eggs and native delicacies from home on summers and weekends.

Should my parents have stopped at three? Fortunately they didn't. My sister—the youngest— is eight years my junior. By the time my siblings and I were out of the family home studying or earning a living in the city, she was the constant companion of my parents. Besides, straight from college and in her first job, she was already sent to Europe to use her programming skills to computerize a university library.

The point I want to make is that any being that takes life in a woman's womb is not a "thing" that can be disposed of easily. What is born is a human resource that has a latent capacity to analyze situations, look for alternatives, and solve problems.

I sincerely believe in the ability of human beings (including the people in Congress) to resolve human—individual and social—problems. To improve the per capita income as a simple arithmetic problem of reducing the denominator (population size) is a no-brainer. To focus on the population, the poor and reproductive right is a worrisome fixation.

There are more challenging solutions if we really want to have "sustainable human development" (Section 2 of the proposed Act). Have we tried combating corruption, improving education standards, increasing job opportunities, upgrading manpower skills, placing stricter controls in our revenue collection system, etc.?

19 RATE PER HOUR

A group of students asked a professor for a consultation time. I overheard the professor replied: "For how long? I am quite busy. I am expensive". I am sure the speaker was just joking, but what was said triggered my reflection for days.

Once, a friend invited me to walk to the shopping mall. As it would take us three-quarter of an hour to reach the destination, I thought about my salary per hour and invited her to take a cab. I would have lost an opportunity to maximize precious minutes to my advantage for a petty cab fare. But I also ignored my friend's peculiar interest for lazy perambulation.

I must admit that like the aforementioned professor, I am also guilty of evaluating alternatives in terms of opportunity costs. An opportunity cost is the amount of income not earned when another course of action is taken. If I am choosing between equally good projects A and B, and I decide for B, there is a corresponding opportunity cost in not choosing A.

The thorny issue appears when you factor in the non-quantifiables in any or all alternative courses of action. For example, in choosing whether I would spend a weekend on a family outing or accept a business engagement, how do I measure the spirit of bonding that could be enhanced by the family outing, or the self-esteem I could build up in the people that matter when I give them my full attention?

The hard part in being an accountant is the tempting ease to look at the material or economic side and the frustration of not feeling your way in feelings as smoothly as you deal with money.

A serious question for my colleague with expensive rate per hour: how much credibility and reputation do you earn when you walk the talk of an open-door policy?

20 SQUARE METER PER PERSON

Space allocation is not exactly the turf of an accountant unless he/she is working for a small company, multitasking in finance, human resource, and building administration. In an organization with greater specialization, the accountant could be asked to give an opinion in proposed standards and guidelines for office space allocation because it involves money. I would like to share an experience that could help the accountant make an informed decision.

A colleague has e-mailed me: "It's another week. I arrived at the office and saw a memo on space reallocation on top of my files. It might be taken up in the next meeting, or so I read. Would I vote for it? Yes, if that is what has to happen. The standards do look neat on paper, 4.5 sq. m. for a cubicle of an assistant professor, 7 sq. m. for a librarian, etc. But in implementation, I can already imagine the grievances.

A boss will complain that he has less space than the staff. A professor will say he has more books than the college's library collection. Someone else might gripe that he has more body mass, receives more visitors, or is more claustrophobic than another person with a privileged bigger office space."

Do you see how a simple space allocation plan can give rise to people management problems? I suggest to the accountant to compute the number of people who will most probably disagree with the plan and multiply this number with their hourly rate. That alone corresponds to downtime in productivity.

What can be done? First, allocate the office space per department and let the department heads decide on the particulars. They know their people better than the planners who might be several floors or buildings away. They can address the reactions and concerns more promptly, if not capably.

Second, allocate on the basis of function rather than persons, their positions, or rank. The office space needed in discharging the function of a manager with 10 direct reports will not be the same as a teacher who shares in a pool of secretarial staff and rooms for student consultations.

Third, consider flexible workspace and plan as many open spaces as possible. It will save you space costs if you do not assign permanent offices to functions that require less presence in the office. In the internet age, the world is an office space.

21 POLITICAL VIEW FOR PHP300

The other day, I left the house at midday. After a few minutes of driving, I saw a good number of men coming out of a little street of tightly cramped houses near a cemetery. When I saw a man leading them with a megaphone and some streamers, I realized they were going towards the rally in the business district. On my way home, I met some traffic jams due to the pedestrians obviously going home from the rally and finding their way to their rented jeepneys which would take them home. A fair day's pay for a fair day's work?

What can you say about getting 300 pesos for joining a political rally one afternoon? "Not bad", says the cab driver I interviewed, "it is better than nothing in these difficult times". And I agreed it isn't really as grueling a task as planting rice to show up in street clothes, hold up a streamer, shout or clap as instructed—all for three to four hours, strictly no overtime.

But then again, I wonder, if the politicians have the money to pay the poor, they might as well give them more concrete tasks during the year like cleaning streets, planting trees, scrubbing pedestrians' walkways, painting public schools, etc. This way, the politicians could earn the votes and not buy them.

Fast forward to five years after this blog entry when I have moved to another city. I was in the gallery in Congress witnessing how they deliberate on the Reproductive Health Law. I was obviously on the wrong side of the gallery, because someone from Congress approached me.

"Whose side are you?" she said, looking at the color of my shirt.

"That side." I pointed towards the opposite area. "But we were not allowed by the guards to enter there."

"You should not be here, or just be careful that those people above you [in the gallery seats above me] might throw stones to you."

I looked up, and I somehow recognized them. They are definitely not from the working middle class. They were the ones who were brought by the service jeepneys that ply the poor districts of a city, before start of the session. Heat went up to my head. If they come on their own accord, the comment that I risk being stoned by them belittles their education and upbringing. And if they come remunerated to support a particular view, the same comment adds insult to injury. P300 is definitely too meager a price for human dignity.

22 BUDGETARY CONTROL

A budget, according to Merriam-Webster dictionary, is "a statement of the financial position of an administration for a definite period of time based on estimates of expenditures during the period and proposals to finance them." The word originated from the French word "bougette" pertaining to a leather bag.

Companies make use of budgets to motivate their people to achieve targets or goals, to have a yardstick to compare actual operations, or to evaluate department managers' performance. It is also used to control activities and expenditures, hence the term budgetary control, for which accountants come in handy.

When budgets are proposed or implemented, the accountants are gatekeepers to the relevant information as to whether proposed budgets are feasible, or actual expenditures deviate from budgetary plans. Thus, accountants can be either loved or hated depending on whether they give a positive vote to a proposed budget or release the approved funds. But sometimes, the accountants are simply ignored depending on how they are perceived by other department heads as possessing political or expert power within the higher echelon of management.

Other departments can also be indifferent to the accounting department if the budgets they implement are not really motivating, or the funds they control have a substitute source. I mused about this organizational reality after coming from a funeral wake—of all places.

Sometime back, I met my teacher in second grade in a wake for a deceased cousin. My former teacher has resigned from my alma mater—a private school— and is currently employed in a public elementary school. Considering that I am also teaching now, as I listened to her, I wondered if I would have the same enthusiasm and energy she still displayed after 30 years in the classroom.

In charge of the outreach skills training for the alumni, their family, and the community surrounding the school, she doesn't have a budget. Armed with a task without any budget, she turned to soliciting donations. Surprisingly for me, she spoke of her fundraising without a tint of self-pity or desperation. She narrated her attempts to get help from the Rotary Club, politicians, local philanthropists, etc.

Then she talked about her actual training offerings which really depended on the survey of participants' needs. It was cooking one time, and handicrafts another time. In business parlance, my teacher knows "pull" instead of "push marketing."

My teacher received letters from beneficiaries, stating how their lives were improved by the training her office provided them. A letter came from Kuwait, expressing gratitude as the skills she learned opened up an opportunity for an overseas job.

I left the wake affirmed that budgets can be handy to motivate people to action, but the lack of approved budgets isn't necessarily a deterrent. The context and constraints within the corporate world can breed "intrapreneurs" who could be saying "give me nothing and I shall get something somewhere else."

I do hope that my fellow accountants realize that what for one person is an instrument for control is for another person a gateway to prove oneself and to insist in achieving a vision that knows no constraints. It's the same reality perceived in two different ways, and thus can give rise to two different behaviors.

Personally, the English word "control" isn't such a positive term. I suggest budgetary negotiation as an alternative. Negotiation conveys a whole gamut of hard and soft skills for the accountants.

23 CONTROL AND RISK

No accountant would want to be out of control (and out of work). In his controlling function, he makes sure that the set objectives are met—from the reorder size for inventory or the collection period for receivables, to the desired year-end profit. The business risks must also be competently controlled. For example, having too much debt is a risk—what if we don't get to pay back our creditors? Having too large an inventory is also risky—what if we don't get to sell them?

The controlling mindset puts a risk to the accountant himself. He has to balance it. Too much control with high risk aversion might exclude him from any entrepreneurial circle of managers as he might just throw cold water on their new business plans. Too little control and high propensity to risk might raise doubt on his job performance.

Fortunately, in an organization with a number of managers who are control freaks, the accountant will just blend with this crowd. But he must remember that he is working with a management team. In that team where everyone is the same, one or more is superfluous. Hence, the accountant reading me now might just as well loosen his control grip to address a team's weak point, and to minimize the risk of being dispensed with. I would like to share this reflection on control:

A project for my students for two semesters was writing any manager of a public or private company. The letter must contain a management problem that is affecting the general public. The letter can be sent to a variety of addresses--city government, village association, fast food owners, shopping center managers, boarding house supervisors, etc.

I got a curious letter from one of the managers who received a letter. She realized that the letter was an academic requirement since the students were pressing her to send a reply. As a suggestion she said that in future projects, I should cue the addressees as regards the responses for the sake of achieving more effectively the course objectives.

Thanks but no thanks. This manager might not have realized it, but the beauty of a field project is that the students are open to all sorts of responses—positive, negative or indifferent. A negation of the students' request for quick official replies would have been already a learning experience in itself. Especially for the grade-conscious, the students will learn that there is a limit to having full control of accomplishments. This applies to cases where a number of factors beyond their classroom performance may influence their grades.

The advantage to the business sector of the letter writing as an academic requirement is the opportunity to improve their systems and processes, to look at the substance of the complaints coming from all sides and not at the motives of their sources, to be confident about their own sincere resolutions of the issues which could obviously be different from the academic perspective.

Most importantly, the virtue of unstructured learning is that it helps students—future employees—prepare to enter a chaotic workplace where even the most controlled, autocratic environment is actually out of control.

24 PLAN TO LOSE

A statement of cash flow is an essential part of any business plan. Quantifying the business concept—market, industry, competition, operations, growth potential—cannot be totally captured in the projected financial statements. Still, the numerical figures must be integrated with all the other plans and their underlying assumptions.

I can understand how a friend could be very nervous when the bank asked her for a statement of cash flow. The figures do not fall down from the sky like shooting stars. They are produced by a lot of thinking, studying, imagining, benchmarking, interviewing, among others.

But there is no preventing anyone from starting with a cash flow forecast using some initial figures at hand. Having the cash needed by the business at any particular time is a good sign of health. And looking at the highs and lows of cash can point out areas for study. These include possible sources of revenue, type of disbursements, nature of business fluctuations, or seasonality.

The danger is the quick-fix mentality: having finished a cash flow forecast, you might abandon tackling a comprehensive business plan. Instead, you can arrive at simplistic action plans to address a cash deficit (get a loan, collect a receivable) or a cash surplus (invest, pay a debt, withdraw capital, purchase a fixed asset, etc.).

In retrospect, I recognized the harm inflicted in teaching how to do a cash flow forecast separate from business planning. I knew more than one manager in class who was dumbfounded when I declared that a business in cash deficit is contributing to the country's poverty. Whatever happened to planning? What use is brain power if it cannot foresee a cash deficit in order to prevent it from actually happening?

Regardless of how many business consultants would affirm that it is normal for a business to experience deficits in the first three years of the business, I say it is not reasonable to assume a losing proposition from the very start. You lose credibility when you cannot pay your suppliers on time. You lose customers when your product goes out of stock. You lose face when you borrow from relatives. You lose serenity when you dip into personal or family savings to pay off a business debt. You lose patience when you argue with other people about money. You get stressed thinking how you will fund the forthcoming payroll.

Reporting a financial net loss in the first 3-5 years of business is another matter. The net loss already includes non-cash adjustments like depreciation of fixed assets or amortization of intangible assets. Thus, a business can experience a net loss without having a cash deficit.

Not being able to recoup your initial investment in the first 3-5 years of business is also another matter. Especially if you report a net loss, there is no "return" to talk about. Your investment or the capital invested has not yielded anything yet when the business has not reported any profit.

I always take this example to personal finance. Applying for a credit card and not having any sound strategy at all to pay the minimum due every month is an attractive proposition only to the credit card company. Who will know? Several entities who offer employment, business, or immigration opportunities do not pay for credit investigations for nothing.

Planning to gain value is food for the brain. Planning to avert a loss at the minimum is an appetizer.

25 ON THE SELF-MADE PERSON AND LEVERAGE

When I was in college, I thought that debt as a financial leverage was a highfalutin idea. But I have come to know it better and simpler.

For the word leverage, think of an ordinary lever which rests on a pivot or fulcrum, and can move heavy objects. For example, if children position a seesaw which is a kind of lever under a mango tree, they can leverage it for easy fruit picking. That is to say, they can surely use its mechanical advantage to gain from it.

Recall the basic accounting equation: asset equals liabilities and capital. It is possible that the assets are 100% invested by the owner. But oftentimes, the business might need more money that can be borrowed from creditors. The amount of equity that the owner has placed in the business can be a leverage to borrow more money. If the creditors see that the owner believes in the business and puts much stake into it, they will most probably lend it money. Then, the debts by themselves can be a financial leverage when the business gets a return on the assets higher than the interest paid on the debts. In layman's terms, you can gain from debts.

I think of friends or network of friends as leverage. Without being a utilitarian, I really believe I cannot exist in this world being alone and using solely my resources. I will need friends to help me out by giving me advice, connecting me to other people who can also assist me, cheering me up, or giving me moral support in an undertaking.

In contrast, I see some people who pride themselves in being self-made, having achieved success by their own efforts and resources alone. I conducted a survey some years back in a class of executives. I asked how much of their career success can be attributed to factors such as friends, family, self, and others. Ninety percent answered "self". Is that a high level of self-esteem, moment of forgetfulness, delusion, or reality? Regardless of the answer, I am convinced that we can ignore an important leverage in indebtedness.

26 GOING CONCERN

When I was an accounting student, I did not easily grasp the phrase "going concern". I initially thought it meant a trouble that will go away soon like a headache.

Accountants are trained to look at a business as a going concern. They assume that it will continue to exist indefinitely. The implication is in the recording and reporting of financial transactions. To wit, assets are not reappraised constantly and recorded at market value but at historical cost instead. Operations are supposed to continue tomorrow in a normal way. The company might experience a liquidity problem today but it is not presumed right away that it will fold up tomorrow. Only when the company is in bankruptcy proceedings does the accountant abandon the going-concern assumption.

In plain English and put in the negative, there should not be any *concern* at all that the business is *going* to fold soon. As an accountant, I should not have any *concern* that my work here is *going* to finish soon. Cheers to continuity, endurance, optimism, and positive outlook!

What can we learn from accounting and the accountants? I know of employees who are constantly applying for work elsewhere from their office desk. Some people who are not vagabonds live in houses where some personal belongings are inside luggages. (I am not referring to summer clothes in winter time or winter clothes during summer.) I speak of persons who have one foot at the door, expecting that anytime a relationship will end. "All my bags are packed, I am ready to go", sings John Denver in "Leaving on a Jet Plane".

At this moment in my musings, my students have disconnected. They do not know John Denver.

27 FULL DISCLOSURE

I hardly take a cab on a holiday but today is one of those exceptions when the whole world seems to think I should have arrived yesterday. The cab driver asked me the introductory question to an anticipated request: how much do you usually pay? I said I take the jeepney and the light rail transit, so I do not know the usual cab fare. Then he requested if I could just add 30 pesos more. I agreed to 20.

Being a bit wary of cab drivers who adjust their rear view mirror to see the passenger, I decided to have a chat with him. First, he offered to bring me to my province – passing through the expressway, meter fare should not exceed 1000 pesos. I replied that the bus would cost me a measly five percent of that figure that "I would rather buy medicines for my mother if I have extra money." I wasn't making it up and he must have sensed it, so he kept quiet.

He then asked me if I own or I rent the place where I stay. That was the time I regretted that I did not bring any pocket book to give the "busy, do not disturb" signal. So to shift the topic, I asked him if he attended the traditional midnight Mass. Unfortunately, he said he got drunk last night (I heard my heart beating twice faster). And perhaps talking more to himself, he said, "I do not think I need to. I can pray here inside my taxi. I do not have the time to go to Sunday Mass." He told me he was actually listening more to another pastor with a radio program, and he might join that pastor's denomination. Fine, I replied, if being a believer in that particular way would make him a better Christian driver, who is doing an honest work and keeping sober, then it would not take long until his entire family will join him.

I might have struck a chord there, since he asked, "Do you think I am doing wrong in asking for an extra charge of P30 earlier?" I told him I agreed to P20 because it is Christmas. He said his reason was the traffic in Manila consumes a lot of gas – cab drivers resort to asking the passengers to reimburse the cost since appealing for higher rates from the government will take ages and are not always effective. I said it is okay for as long as he does not ask an extra charge from every passenger because not every route and day has traffic problems. And it is better if he uses his extra income to buy Christmas gifts for his children rather than buying beer and getting drunk and being happy by himself. He said I was right (that's just to agree at the cognitive level, I have to restrain my rejoicing. Action speaks louder than words, as they say).

We also talked about personal prayer and community worship. At one stoplight, he got his Bible and was looking for that verse which allegedly says that God forbids worship of idols, according to his newly found idol-pastor. The discussion did not go too deep and lengthy. He keeps a picture of his father, whereas I have a picture of Mother Mary, and we both agreed that these are not idols we worship.

Finally, a few meters from my destination, I learned that his real reason for not going to church is the temptations presented by ladies wearing short skirts and the like. So his wife decided they would stop going to Mass. Well in that case, I said it is he and his wife who have to solve this problem between them. Worshipping God for one hour in a week with the entire community of believers is a separate issue that is not even a real matter of contention.

Was he convinced? God knows. But he sounded appreciative and grateful for that Christmas chat. I was also happy to get off at my destination – safely.

28 MATERIALITY AND THE SMALL STUFF

One helpful constraint in Accounting is materiality. If you have a dilemma to include or not a particular financial transaction in the financial statement, you ask yourself: "is this material to this business?" For instance, after closing the books, you discovered that there is double counting of inventory items worth 10,000. The decision to include it will depend on the size of business. If it is San Miguel Corporation, presumably the amount will likely be immaterial because they transact in millions of pesos (i.e. what percentage of their total inventory anyway is 10,000?). If it is a small single proprietorship, omitting this transaction might be a significant understatement of its financial position.

My classmate, Mar, applies the materiality principle to parenting: "For my kids, if it's a small mistake, I just let it pass or else I will have more wrinkles. It is like applying the concept of Accounting, let go of simple and small things, or else you will never finish your audit and you will just get exasperated."

I recalled Richard Carlson's book series *Don't Sweat the Small Stuff.* He warned about focusing on little problems, blowing them out of proportion and losing sight of the bigger picture. The consequences are discontentment, anger, misery or stress. Carlson advised his readers that they have to choose their battles wisely.

I know it is not easy. Wisdom from experience comes in time and after a number of mistakes. One time I really aimed to be precise and I put all the hours in looking for a cash shortage. Then I realized that it was not worth all the energies, and I could have just accounted for the money lost as miscellaneous expense. I just realized that it was not a big deal, after all. Another time, I easily wrote off a debt only to reverse it when the customer showed up and paid.

.

29 RIGHT BRAIN ACCOUNTING

I finished a semester where I lectured on Principles of Accounting II. Giving the final grades four hours after the students handed in their final exams was an all-time high. I usually cram, but with these students I had to constantly monitor how they learn. So I had been updating my grade book from time to time.

Perhaps what helped build the record speed was my special interest to teach accounting (again). At the end of the day, I still love the numbers even if I have already shifted to human behavior topics. Bringing out the accounting tools and concepts from my mental cupboard is like strolling down the memory lane when I spent my first summer in the university doing exercises in journalizing and adjusting entries because the professor in Accounting 1 showed up only twice for the entire semester. (The second time was probably after a group of students reported him to the college secretary.)

The next time I teach accounting, I will have to read more on the learning styles of right-brainers. You see, I began the course using pre-typed transparencies filled with mostly text, interspersed with a few digits. A good number got perfect scores in the quizzes hence, I surmised that the subject was not difficult at all. But some students got low scores in the first of three long exams, and I wondered why. Are they bored with the "texty" slides? I then experimented on abandoning the usual transparencies and making my own—with figures and arrows in every slide.

Thankfully one day, a female student related how she was starting to understand accounting. The previous lessons she said were just Greek to her. A few weeks after that, a fellow approached me after class. He asked if he could go beyond the 16-hour required practicum in accounting offices in local companies. He liked the work experience, even if the accounting jobs were not as advanced as what we discussed in class.

Nonetheless it is not habitual for an accounting professor to assume that there are right-brainers in the classroom. Accordingly I explained a problem again using account names, peso amount, double underlines, and right alignments. Turning my back on the blackboard, behold there were some perplexed faces. A moment's realization and there I was, drawing shapes and connecting them with lines and arrows.

I admit I was a broken record when I would say that the solution was simply logical. Some students retained the expression and repeated it in their final course report. "In accounting, everything is simply logical", objectively perhaps, for the left-brainers. But the right-brainers could not agree until they see the whole picture—creative and intuitive.

I should have shifted to design. Well, that could be my third career shift. I am open to change as it makes life exciting.

30 REMOVAL EXAMS AND PURGATORY

Why do I believe in purgatory?

That's simple. My puny mind of a teacher can think of giving removal exams for students to give them a chance to pass the subject. God must be more merciful.

Removal exams are not for everyone. There are students who really had decided to fail the subject way before the course started. The decision is reflected in their perspective about school, their behavior in class or just going into the class, and their response to warnings in midterm evaluation. To fail them is to give them what they want.

Removal exams are for those who are in the borderline. With a little bit of effort they could have gotten a passing grade. They need not repeat the entire subject. Perhaps personal problems, distractions, or health reasons are the culprit. But overall during the semester, I could see they were running the race and almost got to the finish line before they stumbled.

To give them a passing grade right away is not fair for their classmates who reached the finish line with much more effort, especially if they had the same personal problems.

To give them a passing grade right away is not fair even for themselves. Deep inside, a sincere heart will not enjoy a reward he/she does not merit.

To fail them is cruel because they have exerted the effort. To rank them as failures with those who really ought to be failed (as mentioned above) is a lack of mercy.

Hence, a removal exam is necessary to give them another chance.

I think of purgatory in the same light. There are people who are neither for heaven yet because they are not really very holy. But neither are they for hell yet because they have not really been bad.

31 PARADIGMS AND GOGGLES

Everyone in the accounting profession has shared knowledge and beliefs that will provide the basis for rules about what kind of problems can be dealt with, how it can be solved, what methods are used, or what probable options are available. Merriam-Webster dictionary defines accounting as *"a philosophical and theoretical framework of discipline within which theories, laws and generalizations and the experiments performed in support of them are formulated."*

Luca Pacioli was an Italian friar and mathematician who is generally considered as one of the founding fathers of accounting. Since his time (1445–1517), the accounting paradigm has developed immensely, as indeed an exemplary scientific achievement in organizing the business accounts, determining the quantity of wealth possessed and tracking expenditures at a given time. He also went to great lengths (27 pages!) to expound on bookkeeping. He was also attributed with the advice to merchants and lenders not to sleep until debits had equaled the credits.

Anyone can assimilate the accounting paradigm by inclination, education, experience and exposure. In time and with considerable depth of formation, one will see the world primarily in terms of assets, liabilities, equity, income and expenses. Since the world is much more complex than these categories, the accountant is encouraged to be aware of other kinds of paradigms, avoid a certain professional and potential bias.

I still recall an anecdote I heard years ago about paradigms being associated to goggles. There was a child who was bored with playing in a small swimming pool. His constant clamor to go to the beach has irked his parents that they bought him a pair of goggles that has drawings of colorful sea creatures on them. It changed the world of indoor swimming for the child as he swam among virtual marine life.

In line with that, I realized that it takes little to enter into and enjoy another world—simply wear a different set of goggles. But one should not forget that like the child in the anecdote, there must be a strong desire to try the adventure of other waters. The attitude of open-mindedness facilitates entering into another worldview, seeing the world with another's paradigm. If we cannot risk stepping out of our favored views, then perhaps just taking into consideration that multiple of variety of goggles exists aside from what we are wearing can help minimize biases and give rise to a little more engaging dialogue with people within and outside one's discipline.

32 JEEPNEYS AND ACCOUNTS

Living in a lower-middle class community brings back amusing memories of childhood. I am surrounded by hard-working entrepreneurs selling delicacies, fruits and plants, or buying old umbrellas, pots and pails; children with long faces going to school at the break of dawn; noisy kids playing their hearts out in the streets and under the moonlight; road workers drilling the streets just when everybody would like to sleep; and curious folks throwing litter in your front yard after dark especially when they find it very clean.

A neighbor fondly calls our community the land of the jeepneys—those 16- to 20-seater passenger vehicles inspired by the Japanese jeeps. My street though is not in their route, so pollution from their noxious fumes is minimized. But the queues of parked jeepneys in both sides of the street can pose difficulties for pedestrians and drivers alike. You have to avoid not only the legs of the drivers permanently fixing the bottom of their jeepneys, but also the stray dogs and the children at play.

I am rediscovering jeepneys. It has been a long time since I was a daily commuter. It is a sight to behold the dexterity of the drivers' arms to reach out for the payments from the passengers behind their backs. And they seem to possess high spatial intelligence to remember which hands have paid, which hands are simply passing the money, and which ones need some coins back (i.e. change). It is the passengers who get confused as to whom to give the money that the drivers are passing back.

Not all jeepney drivers are the same, of course. I have seen many drivers who drive more than get bothered with achieving a faultless collection. They do not seem to care much if everyone has actually paid (or perhaps they have a built-in calculator in their heads that tells them "all's paid!").

Some are always looking at their rear view mirror which forces me to pray more that we do not bump the car in front of us. These are the types who literally keep a mental note of faces that look like fare evaders. Others throw short speeches about being honest and paying up. Some smart drivers bring along an assistant to collect the fares, so they can concentrate on driving or getting passengers.

I wonder: whose accounting is more accurate? Who enjoys the workday? However, precision and job satisfaction are not incompatible. We can always work towards balance.

33 POSITION AND COMPETENCE

I often hear the following assumptions from my students in the first weeks of class: "If they are managers, they must be good", and "They would not have been promoted as managers if they were not competent." Fortunately at the end of the semester, more young minds get to think that these are unrealistic assumptions, regardless of whether the cultural context is of high or low power distance.

A friend was offered a promotion from a technical to a managerial position. She asked my advice if she would take the offer. I asked her some questions for reflection: Do you have the training and formation in that higher position? If you will have to train or enroll in a management course and carry out your functions simultaneously, do you have the stamina? Does the company have informal management development programs like coaching and mentoring? She did not take the offer. I know of others who would grab it for the higher salary, perks, and prestige. I also know of another who would not even think and just say, "No, thanks" as she likes the technical part of her job and does not want to relate to people nor deal with people problems. It is a personal choice.

A promotion is a double-edged sword. It can increase your competencies, or it can highlight your incompetence. Authors Peter and Hull coined the "Peter Principle" (1969) to refer to the phenomenon in organizational structures wherein people get promoted to their level of incompetence—the level at which they are incompetent.

The position does not automatically make a person a competent manager. I would even prefer to see a mentally deranged person hurting everyone than an incompetent manager destroying his subordinates' morale and eventually the department's long-term profitability. The first one is obvious—after a time the person is given proper treatment and the problems he created are attended to. The second is like cancer that grows in your body silently and painlessly. You can look healthy for a long period of time, while your body incubates the cancer cells.

A newly promoted manager can still achieve quantifiable outcomes as expected. But failure to develop the competencies to deal with human problems and realities—feelings, emotions, characters, personalities—can lead to low morale, dissatisfaction, team conflicts, etc.

I once knew a technically proficient individual who became a manager with 20 plus direct reports. With all the personnel and relationship problems that his function entails, it became apparent that he could not control his own emotions. He did not even know when he was angry, defensive, or insecure. Other people would label it easily as lack of emotional intelligence. I'd say deadly competence.

34 HIERARCHIES AND AUTHORITY

Accounting forms like petty cash request, check voucher, cash advance liquidation, purchase request need authorization for control purposes. I particularly remember the approval block of many forms I signed as an accounting manager. It contained the fields as low as "Prepared by", "Reviewed by", to as high as "Approved by". But the hierarchy of approvals can go up higher than the accounting manager depending on the nature and amount of transaction.

I also noticed that among my accounting staff, there is one particular person whom everyone consulted for his seniority and experience. There could be times when several employees were gathered round him as he explained "how things are done here." His name did not appear in any accounting form as an authorized signatory but he certainly had some form of authority.

Further, it also happens outside the accounting department. There are persons who do not have any position title but their opinions are respected, their advices are obeyed, their ways are imitated. And there are those persons who have the power of their top positions and they can command anything, but can only gain formal and strict obedience.

A telecommunications company executive, Chester Barnard (1938, *The Functions of the Executive*) proposed a new way of understanding authority back at a period when it was generally accepted to be vested on the managers – their right to be issue commands and be followed. Barnard noted that authority is that character of a communication in a formal organization by virtue of which it is accepted by the workers. Authority is therefore granted by the subordinates to the managers. Managers are forewarned that they have to earn the respect of their subordinates as they do not get a right to it nor earn it automatically.

35 ACCOUNTABILITY

"What is deeply ingrained in you that you think you owe to your Accounting degree?"

That is a tough question. I suppose I am not asked for accounting concepts or principles because there can be days that debits, credits or some accounting concepts do not enter my thoughts. But something that is "deeply ingrained" must really be in me, like dye in a fiber.

So what is it? My answer is sense of accountability.

Accounting gave me the perspective that I should always be accountable – to the company that hired me, the public who relies on my opinions and judgments, my family and friends, even to myself. I do not believe that there is a strict distinction between responsibility and accountability, as if one is responsible if self-motivated, and accountable if subject to control by external forces. I take the simple definition from the dictionary that accountability is "a quality of being accountable, an obligation or willingness to accept responsibility or to account for one's action."

I am also accountable to myself. I will suffer the consequences if I don't take care of myself (like failures or sicknesses). I recall that in the initial stage of studying for the CPA board exam, I decided once and for all not to waste any time and to make sure that I would pass it without any retake. Hence, since I took that decision, I precisely counted the remaining days and hours up to the first day of the examination. I divided the total remaining hours to the different accounting subjects that I needed to master. And every day and every week I accounted for my time by noting how I met my goal of number of study hours per subject. I thought I owed it to myself not to prolong or repeat the hardships (mental, physical and emotional) of reviewing for the board exam.

When I started working as an accountant, I also felt accountable to myself. It is because I knew that if I did not record the entries correctly in the journal, I will spend a lot of time balancing the ledger, reviewing what I did, making reconciling or adjusting entries, and the like.

Hence, I do not take accountability as a form of external control. It is not as if I were less free if I make myself accountable to something or somebody. Being accountable was a chance to learn more – to aim higher because I can exceed my last performance, to strive above real or imagined dissatisfactions (mediocrity being one of them), to do better because I can, to excel because God did not create me for something less.

And because it is a learning process, accountability suggests openness to others. And in the case of accounting, "others" means everyone with a stake in the accounting profession—students, professionals in private, public and government practice, accounting teachers, the general public. This little book is a testimony of what accounting is for me and my life. I sincerely wish I am able to share something helpful. Let me know.

M.V.Q.C.
Pasig City, 20 September 2013